WORLD RAT DAY

Poems About Real Holidays You've Never Heard Of

J. Patrick Lewis

Illustrated by Anna Raff

Candlewick Press

For Bev and Rocky, who made every day a holiday
J. P. L.

For Jean, who would be thrilled her prediction came true
A. S. R.

Text copyright © 2013 by J. Patrick Lewis
Illustrations copyright © 2013 by Anna Raff

"Paddy Pork" first appeared in *Snuffles and Snouts,* edited by Laura Robb, New York: Penguin Putnam/Dial: 1995.
"A Flamingo" and "Jack A." copyright © 1990 by J. Patrick Lewis.

First edition 2013

Library of Congress Catalog Card Number 2012942612

ISBN 978-0-7636-5402-3

LEO 17 16 15 14 13 12
10 9 8 7 6 5 4 3 2 1

Printed in Heshan, Guangdong, China

This book was typeset in Gill Sans.
The illustrations were made from ink washes and drawings, assembled digitally.

Candlewick Press
99 Dover Street
Somerville, Massachusetts 02144

visit us at www.candlewick.com

CONTENTS

January
2
Happy Mew Year
for Cats Day

A TOAST TO MY CAT

On Mew Year's Day,

Let my cat be

The Queen of Purriosity

And play loud mewsic,

Spin a yarn,

Join the party in the barn,

Eat Mice Crispies,

Drink eggnog . . .

And hog the bed before the dog!

EIGHT TABLE MANNERS FOR DRAGONS

At every meal, bow your head, fold your wings, and say "Graze."

Wait till someone screams, "Let's heat!"

Don't talk with people in your mouth.

Never blow on your soup. That only makes it hotter.

Don't smoke.

Never remove a hare from your food.

Play with your food, but don't let it run around screaming.

Chew your food. Once.

January
16
Dragon
Appreciation Day

HiPPO
DRONES

4

WHY I'M LATE FOR SCHOOL

This hippopotamus thinks I'm a stool.

I wish he'd let me up to go to school.

If he squatted on my finger or one hand,

One knee or elbow, I could understand.

But head to toe? That makes it awful hard

To have a conversation with the lard!

Though not as hard as telling Mr. Bruce,

My teacher, the old-hippo-on-the-loose-

Who's-flattened-my-whole-body's my excuse!

PADDY PORK

Paddy Pork
  wakes at nine,
    steps across
      the other swine.

Trots to market,
  buys an ax,
    lugs it home
      in paper sacks.

Paddy heaves-
  ho—high!
    Heavens, how
      the chips fly!

Piggies, hens,
  and roosters stop,
    watching Paddy
      Pork chop.

March
1
National
Pig Day

ROBIN
(turdus migratorius)

WHAT THE WORM KNOWS

Take my advice:
For your own good,
Stay away from
The Robin 'hood.

March
15
Worm Day

THE RAT IS

the
mous-
tache
in
the
trache,

the
wrong-
doer
in
the
soer

10

April

4

World Rat Day

11"

9"

7"

3"

11

A THOUSAND BABY STAR

When I was ten, I ran to catch
A baby star that leapt
Among the trees, a dime of light
I cupped and capped, and kept.

How could I ever catch them all
As they were getting ready
To fire up a festival?
ELECTRIFIED CONFETTI.

BATS

Upside-down sleepers
Awaking in waves
Are Sweepers of Twilight
And Keepers of Caves

Black sacks in the morning
Airmailed at night
Dispatchers of insects
In boomerang flight

Brushed hushes are not
Evening's violin strings
But murmurs to moonbeams
And whispers on wings

April
17
Bat Appreciation
Day

13

A BULLDOG IS

A perfectly lovely

Excuse for a pet

A face you remember

To never forget

A sieve for the slobber

A soloist (grunts)

The sumo of canines

The semi of runts

A growl that must frighten

Away his dog fleas

The model for numerous

Small SUVs

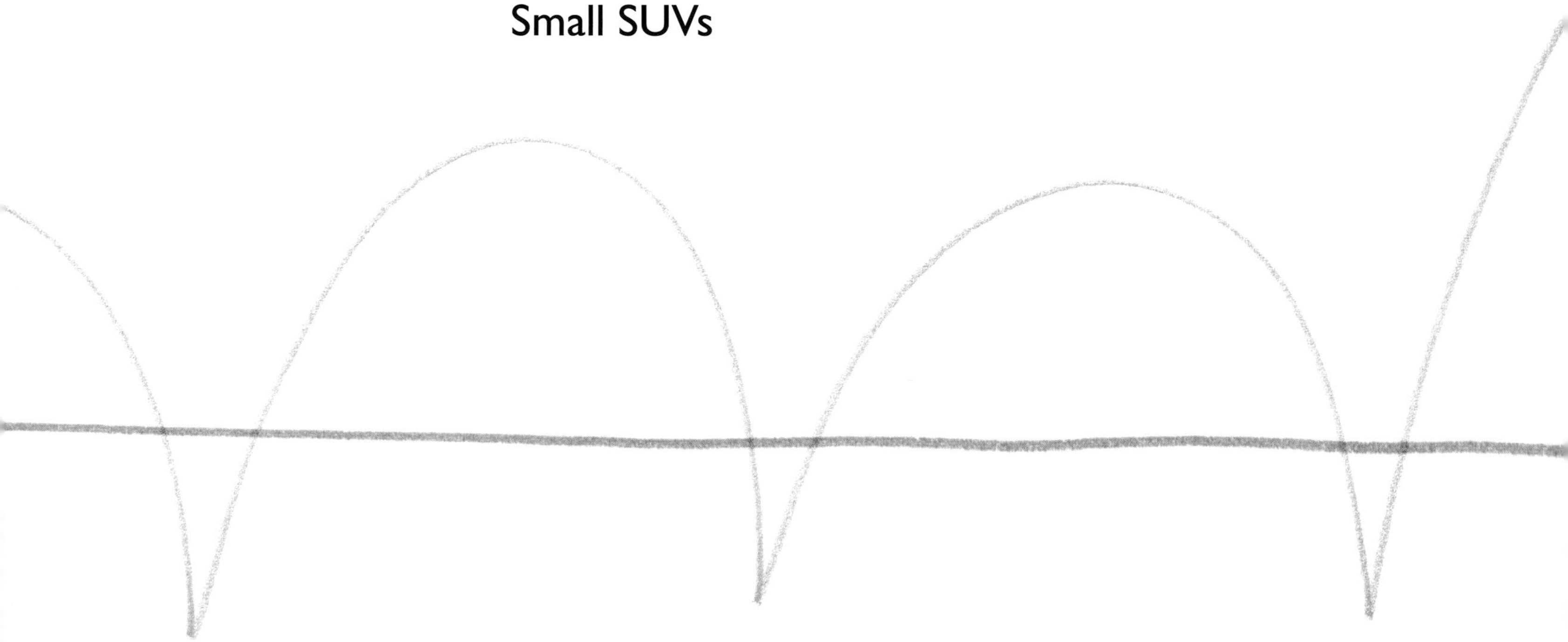

A bowlegged, waddling
Disaster zone
The reason you'd never
Leave him home alone

THE HIP

A centipede said on vacation,
"Don't bug me—I'm into gyration.
    And when I go on trips
    I'm so hip that my hips
Hula hundreds of times in rotation."

THE FOOT

Come thunder and lightning and hail,
One can always depend on the mail,
    But it won't be on time
    If it's dragged through the slime
By a one-footed mailman snail!

THE BUTT

A mother baboon is a beauty,
Her baby baboon is a cutie
    And the whole baboon troop
    Starts to whistle and whoop
When the baby starts shaking her booty.

THE FLIPPER

Since the penguin was missing a part
(Doctors noticed no knees on her chart),
    Someone said, "Let's equip her
    To flap with a flipper—
A butler with wings." Pretty smart!

May 12 Limerick Day

THE PAW

Do you know what makes grizzlies unique?
It's their paw power, not their physique.
    Sort of like rocket science—
    One boost from those giants
Could knock someone into next week!

SAID THE FROG

I was really in a muddle
looking over a mud puddle
'cause I didn't have a paddle
or a twig to ride the reef.
But I said, "Oh, fiddle-faddle,
this is just a little piddle
of a second fiddle puddle."
So I saddled up a leaf.
I set sail on the puddle,
but I reached the muddy middle
and I rocked the leaf a little,
then I gave it all I had.
And I solved the mighty riddle
of the whole caboodle puddle
when I hopped up on the middle
of a beetle launching pad.

20

THE MATA MATA

What's the matter with a mata
mata turtle?
Well, the face for one thing is a
major hurtle.
No, I don't think I'm exagger-
ating, am I,
when I say one look from him
could stop a semi?
It's as if a mask worn by a
hockey goalie
had been plastered on with lumpy
guacamole.
Yet a mata mata is a
handsome creature
to a turtle turtle with this
feature feature.

A Flamingo is a loooooooooool drink of something Pink

WITH NUTS ONLY

You enter his arena
From here to Pasadena
And laugh like a hyena—
A cobra will not budge.

You wave a red bandanna
From here to Indiana,
Or dangle a banana—
He's sober as a judge.

Since the time of Noah,
A cobra's like a boa,
And neither one will go a-
Way till you say

"Fudge!"

June
2
Yell "Fudge!" at
the Cobras in
North America Day

June
14
National
Skunk Day

If the skunk did not exist,
Then the skunk would not be mist.

Eau de
Eeeew!

July
14
Ohio Sheep
Day

THE BAH BAH BAHS

No one will ever forget Ewe.

28

COW DREAMS

Cows that stand in farmers' fields
Promise tons of sunny yields.

Cows that belly down in shade
Promise showers, I'm afraid.

Cows that give the moon a moo
Wait for starlight, then give two.

Cows that fall asleep and dream
Dream the moon is pouring cream.

July
15
Cow Appreciation
Day

THE RHI-NOSE-EROS

I'll tell you if you promise
Not to gossip it about:
The nose of the rhinoceros
(Rhi-NOSE-eros's snout)
Isn't made of Play-Doh, mud,
Aluminum, or tin.
It isn't wrapped in grocery bags,
Wet paper towels, or skin.
A rhi-NOSE is a compass
That is Rhino's point of view—
You wouldn't want to be there
If it's pointing straight at you.
He follows where it leads him
Like a map made out of bone.
A rhino knows he chose the nose
That grows just like Pinocchio's
And ends abruptly, I suppose,
At rhiNO PARKING ZONE.

September
22
World Rhino
Day

WHAT ARE THE CEPHALOP-ODDS?

I wish I was an octopus
In inky-dinky weather.
Then you and I could octopush
Our suction cups together.

October
8
International
Cephalopod
Awareness Day

32

October
26
Mule Day

JACK A.

The donkey is an ani-mule
Who won't put up with ridi-cule.
His temper's short and, as a rule,
He's seldom very tame.

Especially if he's called Old Zack
Or Shorty Horse or Prickleback.
And if, of course, you call him Jack,
Don't mention his last name.

33

THREE-TOED SLOTH

He bats around a luna moth,
He counts up all his toes,
He wears the smile of the sloth
That everybody knows.

He races to the tallest limb—
.16 miles per hour
(The fastest ever time for him),
And looks down from his tower

In the rain forests above Brazil
To watch the world below.
If he could speak, the sloth would shout
From all the treetops . . . WHOA!

November
19
National
Sloth Day

FINISH

34

CHOCOLATE-COVERED ANTS

You start with that ant mandible—
Completely understandable—
    A chocolate jaw has never tasted sweeter.

Then bite a bit of abdomen
Before you've finally grabbed a min-
    i-leg, an itty-bitty centimeter.

But ants despise this holiday
That is their grand finale day
    When you become the Chocolate Anteater.

December
16
Chocolate-Covered
Anything Day